2001

2001

Paschal Magro OFM Conv

The Tomb of Saint Francis

The series of colour plates in this volume with a relative
extensive study by Gerard Ruf OFM Conv have been
edited in German by HERDER EDITORS, Freiburg-
Basel-Wien, in 1981.

Paschal Magro OFM Conv

The Tomb of Saint Francis

Thè celebration of the Saint
in the Frescoes of the Lower Church

Casa Editrice Francescana - Assisi (Italy)

1182-1982
The Friars Minor Conventual of the Basilica of
Saint Francis in Assisi on the VIII CENTENARY
OF THE BIRTH OF THE SERAPHIC FATHER.

To The Reader

The following pages don't aim at offering the reader an exhaustive word on the historical formation of the Lower church of San Francesco in Assisi.

They rather aim at informing about the intentions of the founders and patrons who with the spacious crypt intended mainly to create an intimate space that could urge his heart and mind in a personal dialogue with the Saint buried there below and whose heavenly glory the architectural lines of the triple church, the mural and stainedglass texts proclaim.

The Tomb of the saint alone can't give the visitor an adequate comprehension of all the meanings insinuated in the enchanting language of art.

One should consider also the development the new historical situations of the Franciscan Order have imposed on the conscience of the patrons whether friars or not.

That's why the shrine doesn't remain just the sign of the "glory of the blessed corpse" (A. venturi) but becomes necessarily the veichle of the ideal and practical choices of the "mystical body" of the Poverello constituted by his spiritual family in perennial and always more lively leavening.

The founder Gregory IX endowed the Sepulchre-church with the title of "Head and Mother" of the Franciscan order, a title once reserved to the Lateran church in Rome. This stressed the "special" physical and spiritual presence of Saint Francis, the penitent man whom Innocent III had dreamt of as the saviour of that church.

It is more than natural, so, that all events of the franciscan family — those serene and others less so — could find echo in the pictorial text that enwraps the body of the Father and Brother as with "canopies and silken palls" (Mirror of perfection, 109).

As if to entrust them to his protection and blessing and, at the same time, to fix them in colours in order to share their knowledge, anxieties and hopes with the pilgrim throngs visiting the main Franciscan Shrine.

The friar author

INDEX

1. The sepulchre-church: an eminent sign of the glory of the Saint and privileged place of grace

From its very beginnings the basilica of Saint Francis in Assisi was expressly meant to be a sepulchre-church: "It has seemed to us convenient and praiseworthy that for reverence towards the same Father a special church should be built in which his body could find definite burial"[1].

As such the Church had its primitive models in the Tomb churches of martyrs and confessors of faith built by Constantine the Great in the IV Century.
The functional aspect of the Church of San Francesco in Assisi as an earthly sign of the heavenly glory of the saint buried in its bowels was suggested and supported by the same companions of him: "Blessed Giles held that on his body a remarkable church should be built so that it could insinuate, in the rude minded people, the idea of his eminent holiness"[2].

With the solemn canonization on the primitive tomb in the church of Saint George in Assisi (July 16, 1228), Gregory IX had inaugurated the liturgical celebration of Francis. With the laying and blessing of the first stone on the "Hill of hell" to the West of the city, the day after, he was officially giving start to the artistical one[3].

Why did the civil and ecclesiastical authorities decide to build the Sepulchre of Saint Francis outside the city of Assisi, one might ask. Why didn't they destroy Saint George's church to build over such new Sepulchre as afterwards they will decide to do for the twin Tomb of Saint Clare?

Traditional cultural schemes help already to offer a first answer to the topographical question: "The *martyrium* (witness church) and the cemetery were usually built outside the city. Saint John Chrysostom begins his sermon by explaining why the liturgical assembly takes place in an out of reach building and in that exact day. «Why today?» he asks. «Because today we celebrate the memory of the Cross. Why outside the city? Because the Lord was crucified outside the city of

Jerusalem. Why did our ancestors want to come together in this place and not in another? Because here a great number of dead are buried»"[4].

But an adequate answer can be found in the same ascetical christian way of thinking and behaving of Francis of Assisi. Following the inspiration of his minstrel-like mystical customs, he once obliged his friars to drag him naked up to the stone on which they used to pillory evil-doers on the square of the Palace of the Consuls in Upper Assisi[5]. By doing so, he intended to give himself and all spectators a lesson on mortification, on love for prisoners and on the imitation of Christ who for our love was mocked and hanged between two thieves outside Jerusalem.

The episode in the version of Saint Bonaventure's *Legend Major* throws not a little light on the real motivations of the topographical choice of the definitive Tomb. Only Bonaventure tells us that Francis didn't address the people from the stone pulpit reserved for preachers in the Cathedral square *but from the stone pedestal where they used to punish publicly evil-doers*. If, so, it was his deep veneration for the holy Eucharist that had made him express the wish to die in France since he had admired French people's eucharistic passionate piety; if it was the nostalgia for the heroic beginnings of his Gospel adventure that made him close effectively his days at the Portiuncola Convent[6]; it was his admirable but inimitable humilty, the imitation of Christ and the love for criminals that had pushed him to choose the gallows hill as his burial place!

This is what a local Threehundred literary source expressly says: "When the holy Father was nearing his end, his companions asked him: Where would you like to be buried? And he answered: Where the gallow for evel-doers is. Which desire was afterwards fulfilled, since where is now the main altar of the Church, there was formerly the place of justice"[7]. When still alive, Francis was aware of the jelousy his fellow citizens already had and will have still more had for his bodily relics. No place on earth could have robbed such a glory to the city that had given him birth[8].

Gregory IX had entrusted the organization of the work of the building of the Sepulchre-church to the genial Brother Elias of Assisi. With the Comacini masters he is considered to be the main architect of the famous artistic complex consisting of a triple church, papal house and convent for friars[9].

Today's lower church was meant to be the capacious Cript (Figg. 1-2), while the upper church was the real monastic church. Both churches resulted an artistic crown of glory on the Cell of memory that held the stone casket with the precious treasure of the relics of Saint Francis.

10

F. PROVIDONI (1704): Reconstruction of the "Hill of hell" with the gallow. In 1230 Gregory IX rebaptized it "Hill of Paradise".

The difficulties arising from the sloping and precipitous site of the hill didn't block the strong willed Elias from completing the essential structures of the shrine in 1239, the day stamped on the oldest bell in the tower[10].

From the beginning, christian pilgrims looked at the Church of San Francesco as one of their beloved and penitential ports. The bishop of Pisa Federico Visconti had to say of it (1260-70): "The man of spirit has to lead the sinner to confession and to make amendment for his sins. So he has to induce him to perform works of penitence such as going on pilgrimage to the Tomb of Christ or that of Saint James in Compostella or that of Saint Peter in Rome or that of Saint Francis in Assisi. Count if you can the men and the women that have visited the Church of San Francesco in Assisi, in view of the remission of their sins! And rightly, since glorious appears the saint in our days and since glorious and most beautiful and capacious is his church which our Lord Pope Innocent IV has endowed and enriched with great priveleges and many treasures. And so has churches dedicated to so many saints be: that every heart rejoices in going, in remaining and in returning often to them"[11].

2. Central nave of lower Church:
the conformity of Saint Francis with the suffering Christ

The main body of the lower Church forms the corridor that takes to the altar of the Tomb that emerges from the dark background of the low apse. This space reserved for the assembly originally received light from romanesque windows on the side walls. The iconographical mural message resulted more readable then since it was easier reached by the light sources, now pushed to the exterior walls of the side chapels built towards the end of the XIII century.

The pilgrim, already charmed by the magical powers of the polychromatic vaults and walls, had then to assimilate their ideal religious contents and encounter the saint in his real christian greatness and acknowledge his thaumaturgical presence.

Towards the middle of the century, the friars represented on the parallel walls the "Conformitas of Francis with Christ". Francis' imitation of the Crucified Master had reached its apex in the impression of the stigmata on Mount La Verna. Brother Elias who was acting as Vicar of the Order at the Saint's death, had solemnly written: "I announce to you a great joy, an extraordinary miracle. The world has never heard of such a portent but in the Son of God who is Christ the Lord. Sometime before his death, our Brother and Father appeared crucified, bearing the five wounds that are the true stigmata of Christ impressed in his body"[12].

Such noble and moving news the parallel walls that run towards the Tomb had to continue to echo to the pilgrim and visitor.

Built up only between the persons of Christ and Francis of Assisi and not between the single episodes, the glorifying comparison is so developed:

COMPASSION OF FRANCIS (left wall)	PASSION OF CHRIST (right wall)
Francis disinherited	Christ undressed
Francis saves Lateran Church	Christ crucified
Francis preaches to birds	Christ taken from cross
Francis stigmatized	Christ buried
Francis dead and Mourned	Christ ?

The opening of the side Chapels in later years produced fatally the mutilation of the two cycles, the very first to illustrate openly and determinately the eulogy, neither easily mint nor always irenically accepted owing to the audacity in presenting so close to one another the two religious figures. If on one side there was the risk of undervaluating the person of Christ, on the other there was the one of over-valuating that of Francis.

From the tough pillars that rhyme the central aisle in three equal bays, there sprut festive and iridescent ribs. High on the vaults these become floreal frames to the azure sectors of sky, strewn with stars realized with tiny semispherical mirrors, that twinkled through the reflection of the thousand trembling flames in the numerous wrought-iron chandeliers. It is not difficult to see - at the beginning of the artistic fervour linked with the saint that, as an itinerant apostle, had lived a unique brotherly relationship with the natural environment - the will of the friars to reproduce accurately the wonder of the same saint for the "serene air", the "bright precious and beautiful stars", the "colourful flowers and herbs".

G.B. MARIANI (1820): The architectural triptych forming the Basilica of San Francesco. A. Venturi defined it as the "most beautiful house of prayer the world boasts of".

15

3. The altar on the Tomb: "Francis is here!"

In the building logic of paleo-christian sepulchre-churches, in between the arch of the apse and the main aisle, one had to find the *Cell of memory*.

This consisted in a quite small chapel, normally hewn in the rock and served to hold the stone or marble casket with the relics of the Confessor or Martyr of faith. This underground memorial was crowned by the altar that for the assembly represented the liturgical climax. It also represented the goal and the source of grace longed for by the pilgrim in his tiring way towards the shrine (Fig. 18).

The Altar of the Tomb of Saint Francis was realized in gothic style by Comacini masters and decorated with mosaics by Cosmatesque ones (Fig. 57). All these artists have held in due consideration the insistent will of the Saint who always wished to see precious ornaments in the altar[13]. For the pilgrims who gave end to their pilgrimage at the foot of the altar, the small oil lamps between the columns were visible voices that whispered with their trembling flames: "Francis is here!".

A painting on wood of the XIII Century (now in the Museum of the Basilica) represents it as the goal of sick and afflicted people, imploring the intercession of the miracle-worker. This is also what a contemporary miniature in a Basilica choral code is representing[14].

An iconostasis of the same cosmatesque artistic manners of the altar once separeted the presbytery and choir reserved for the clergy from the nave space reserved for the assembly. Dismantled later on, it has been rebuilt in a choristery with a small pulpit under the Chapel dedicated to Saint Stanislaus Martyr near the altar (Fig. 15).

Various tamperings on the original walls in the bays next to the altar, witnessed by shelves and mural sacraria, reveal architectural events, still very mysterious to the same scholars of the Basilica (Figg. 13-14).

Since the saint's definitive burial on the 25th May 1230, this area had become the epicentre of all movements in the glorious history of the Tomb of Saint Francis. Security reasons in times of war that exasperated fanaticisms dangerous to the relics of the Saint, compelled Eugene IV (1442) and Sixtus IV (1476) to render impraticable the tiny chapel under the altar.

In 1818, during the excavations intended to bring back to light the urn with the relics, the original structures were unfortunately destroyed. Today one can reconstruct them ideally if one looks to the Assisi tomb of Saint Clare; the Chapel of the memory was here luckily preserved, when after having undergone more or less the same manumissions of that of Saint Francis, was also brought back to the original state of practicability, in 1850[15].

Between 1818 and 1824, Pasquale Belli developed the old underground cell in a more capacious Cript in neo-classical style. In the years 1927-32, Ugo Tarchi undressed the walls from the XIX Century sumptuous marbles and clothed it with the evocative rough pink stone of Assisi in neo-romanesque tastes.

The first followers of the Saint still gravitate around their Master whom Dante Alighieri defined as the "mystical Sun of the World": Friars Leo, Rufinus, Masseo and Angelo, the noble and the pious roman lady "Brother Jacopa", in the new Crypt; Bernard, Sylvester, Electus, Valentine, William... still in the right arm of the transept of the Lower church where the other above mentioned brothers were also buried until 1932.

The Tomb of Saint Francis was the mystical goal of a miraculous visit by Saint Clare, seriously ill at San Damiano, on Chrismas Night 1252[16]. In 1291, during a pious pilgimage to the shrine of the Saint, blessed Angela of Foligno had a strong mystical experience, wich she describes in her spiritual diary[17].

Just from the beginning of its history, the Sepulchre-church was looked at as the absolute spiritual pole of all truly franciscan souls.

4. The transept: St. Francis "Another Christ" and "Angel of VI apocalyptic seal"

When Francis was sick guest in the Palace of Bishop Guidus the Second of Assisi, he had predicted the future glorification christians would have reserved to his stigmatized body. The frescoe decoration of these vaults, realized by the friars on the falling of the First Centenary from the death of the Founder (1310-1330), well fulfills the prophecy of the Saint[18].

In all the history of art there is no body of works of art that could match the one here in the genial organic articulation of the ideas it is conveying.

The whole decoration consisting of three main sections, unbinds from the centre to expand itself organically towards the extreme ends of the right and left arms of the transept; it is meant to celebrate the christlike person of the Saint buried below, and at the same time, to illustrate the salvific role he had for that epoch, so much nostalgic of a new history as deeply anguished by apocalyptic future visions.

A. The cross-vault and apse:
the eschatological beatitude of Francis

An allegorical, didactic composition was reserved by the friars for these main decorative spaces that enwrap the Tomb-altar below. The pictorial text had to illustrate the heavenly glory of Francis obedient, poor and chaste, victorious over vices contrary to these virtues.

This spiritual franciscan warfare (deriving evidently from the traditional *Psychomachìa*) is built up with elements of greek mythology and philosophy as well as christian theology and franciscan history. It makes the observer remember the moral message the franciscan preaching had to propose according to the indications of the IX Chapter of the Rule: the friars had to proclaim "vices and virtues, pain and glory". The theme that celebrated Francis and his friars as "athletes against the antichrist" findable in the writings of chronicler Jacques Vitry when Francis was still living, is here sharpened by the apocalyptic decoration in the ribs that frame the "sails" and the lost fifth allegory of the "Glory of the Crucifix" in the apse-cap. Representing Revelation book figures and symbols, it related the theme of the simple eschatological warfare of the Goespel to its supreme biblical model: the apocalyptic universal Judge (Fig.17.

It is impossible, at this point, to ignore the diametrically opposed interpretation given to this franciscan "manifesto". One can say that it was mainly intended for the friars gathered in the choir: the topographical disposition of the apocalyptic decoration of the ribs obliges one to read it from the apse!

Observing the representation of Francis beardless and dressed as deacon as well as the polychromatic splendour of the vaults, somebody attributed the figurative schemes to the official and moderate wing of the order: the "Comunity"[19]. Others, on the contrary, have seen schemes and ideas dear to the polemical and extremist wing of the "Spirituali". Since the fourth decade of XIII Century, for apologetical and pretextuous reasons, these rigorists had mint the alarming and daring image of Francis "Apocalyptic angel of the sixth seal" (Apoc. 7).

The anticurial and anticomunitarian dimension of such an image has pushed someone to write that in the Assisi official seat of the Order "badly suited perhaps the franciscan «Comunity»"[20]. But any unilateral interpretation seems to lack of realism and historical knowledge. The beardless Francis has nothing to do with contestation phenomenons on contemporary social and political scene; it is simply derived from the allegorical images of Christ, beardless "Sheperd", "Soldier" and "Ephebus" of paleo-christian art[21]. The image of Saint Francis as the apocalyptic angel, expurgated of its messianic joachite aspect already since Saint Bonaventure's generalate (1263), had become an hagiographical heritage of the official wing of the Order too[22]. In the explosive years of the decoration, finally, the two wings of the Order, had come closed to each other to defend the same pauperistic positions against what now was considered a *common evil*: the "heretic" John XXII[23].

This irenic and concordist interpretation obliges then to suppose if not to hold that the iconographical programme couldn't be free of traces, especially from Vienne Council on (1311), of the "resistence" of *all the Order* against the conciliar and papal declarations on individual and comunitarian poverty.

In this historical environment, the centrality of the allegory of poverty is unquestionable given its frontal position as regards friars in the choir-stalls. It found its countertheme in the "Gloriosus Franciscus" according to an eschatological scheme suggested by the liturgical antiphon borrowed from the Office of Saint Martin of Tours: "Francis poor and humble on earth, enters rich in heaven, honoured with celestial hymns". So also the frontality (always as regards friars in the choir) of the two Angels with the stigmata, in the ribs (Figg. 62-63), insinuating the stigmatized Saint Francis, supports the autoglorificative reading of all this decoration that found its climax in the allegorical crucified Lamb of God in the apse[24].

Angelo Clareno, the most indomitable of the excomunicated Fraticelli, daringly paraphrasing a biblical messianic page (Hebrews, I, 1) preached and wrote: "At various times in the past in various ways Christ spoke to us through the fathers, the apostoles, the prophets, the martyrs, the doctors and all the saints; the last days he spoke to us through his son Francis, the Son that has appointed to inherit all future things (...). Dress on the same feelings of Obedience, Poverty and Chastity of the blessed Francis, who in his conformity with the Crucified Christ, humbled himself (...). For this reason, Christ raised him high and gave him the name which is the above mentioned Francis, Lamb and Word made flesh (...), and in all of you we saw his glory of almost the Firstborn of Father Jesus Christ, full of grace and sanctity"[25].

Could one read and understand the allegorical text of the cross-vault and apse outside this nearly idolatrous order of ideas?

The pilgrims to the Tomb, raising their eyes towards these breathtaking vaults of Paradise had to be able to exclaim: "We can see his glory...!"

B. The arms of the transept: the roots of franciscan "Sequela Christi"

The above analysed glorious image of the Saint finds its articulated development in the representation of its historical and theological roots on the barrel-vaults of the two arms of the transept: the episodes of the Infancy and Passion of Christ gospels.

The image of the historical Christ, of God born of a woman, was mainly a spiritual conquest of lay evangelism at the dawn of our millenium. This is the image that radically supports the contemplative and active faith of Francis and his Order. "He would recall Christ's words through persistent meditation and bring to mind his deeds through the most penetrating consideration. But above all the humility of the *Incarnation* and the charity of the *Passion* were so deeply impressed in his memory that he wanted to think of hardly anything else"[26].

A)   RIGHT ARM THE INCARNATION OF THE WORD. The theme in the central "sails" is inserted into that of the historical infancy of Jesus *through the allegory of Chastity*. The eschatological bliss of pure of heart Francis is comprehended in the gospel schemes of spiritual infancy or adoption in Christ. The iconographical detail of the baptism in the allegory is the evident hint for this ideal connection. "Having a firstborn Son - Saint Augustine writes - God made him son of man; and so, conversely, he rendered the son of man, son of God"[27]. The spiritual infancy biblical truth had found an exceptional stained-glass expression in this Assisi art atelier since tens of years. It is the only time that the "confrmitas Christi" is expressed in the Christ-Francis infancy terms (and not in the Christ Passion-Francis compassion ones): to Christ babe on the womb of Mary corresponds Francis physically adult but baby-like held by Christ. In 1291 Angela of Foligno was shocked by the unique spiritual charm emanating from the window in the Upper church.
Returning to our theme in the Lower church, under the Incarnation cycle, one finds two episodes (developed in three frescoes) regarding infants in difficult situations and commended to the intercession of Francis (Figg. 50-53).
One can't beleive in the pure casuality of such themes, excluding all intention of art patrons to include them in the general theme of infancy developed in this area.
On the leitmotiv of infancy they have dedicated and decorated the adjacent Chapel in memory of Saint Nicholas of Bari, patron saint of children (the Christmas Santa Klaus) and adolescents - without excluding still to be proved piety motives towards the Saint of the Roman patrons of the Chapel, the noble Orsinis.
As regards the very famous Cimabue's Madonna with Child, Angels and Saint Francis (Fig. 32), one can't reasonably consider it an integral part of the decorative programme of the right transept. It's what is left over of an earlier decoration begun without precise programming.
The same might be affirmed of the remaining decorative bands representing mainly franciscan figures (Figg. 35-39), unless one wants to link them with the theme of the spiritual filiation of Francis, further development of the spiritual infancy one.

B)   LEFT ARM : THE PASSION OF CHRIST AND COMPASSION OF SAINT FRANCIS. The àllegorical celebration of the Saint in the central "sails", to the south, is inserted in the schemes of the Passion of Christ and compassion of Saint Francis (Figg. 19-31, 33), through the allegory of Obedience. A well-known branch of the Letter to the Philippians inspires and founds biblically such connection of ideas: "Jesus Christ became obedient even to accepting death, death on a cross. But God raised him high and gave him the name which is above all other names so that all beings in the heavens, on earth and in the underworld, should bend the knee at the name of Jesus..."[28].

The iconographical detail of the Crucifix on the wall behind the figure of Obedience and that of the kneeling angels - findable only in this allegory - don't leave any doubt about the real intention of the friars to unite organically the two groups of frescoes.

Spaccato sulla linea in pianta A.B.

The architect of the Tomb of Saint Clare followed the model of that of Saint Francis. The design shows how the former looked like before 1850 when the actual spacious crypt was built. The reconstruction of the Tomb of Clare shown above is from F. CASOLINI, *Il protomonastero di S. Chiara,* Milano 1950, p. 216.

If in the North transept art leads spiritually the visitor to the contemplation of Betlehem, in the South one it invites him to the contemplation of Golgotha and La Verna, the mount where Francis was stigmatized. In Franciscan ambiences, pictures and cycles of the Passion are always integrated with protagonists of franciscan history.

In our case, panels 26 and 31 are meant to be parallel and have to be read together. The large Crucifixion - seriously mutilated in 1623 - was the only one here lacking of a franciscan presence. Lodovico da Pietralunga (+ 1580) assures us that at the feet of Christ Crucified there were only soldiers casting dice on the tunic of Christ:[29] Francis of this Golgotha was just that of the parallel frescoe on the opposite wall.

The mural triptych with the Madonna affectionately asking Jesus in her arms to bless Francis before John the Evangelist on account of his superior spiritual and physical resemblance with him suffering, can be read both after the above said combination Golgotha-Verna and at the end of the whole Christian and Franciscan cycle, as a corollary (Fig. 33).

If John the beloved apostle found place "near" Jesus on the Cross, Francis of Assisi found it "in" the same wounded heart of Him: this is what a homily of Gregory IX held in Assisi on October 4, 1235 had hinted at and what has certainly inspired the frescoe that glorifies the saint as morally greater than the apostles (Lc. 22, 24)[30].

The small frescoe with Judas hanging from a beam has to be associated with that of Francis victorious over Death represented by the strangely dressed skeleton wearing a tumbling crown, in the parallel, analogous space in the north transept (Figg. 25 and 49). No one should object to such a reading; the same topographic leap runs between the two roundels under the arches of the gates that take to the cloister of Sixtus IV. These are conveying the two combined images of Christ and Francis in the act of disclosing their side and hand wounds.

No one, anyhow, should exclude a possible relation of the same two figures with the Crucifixions on the opposite walls (Figg. 26 and 34). In this case they are signifying: Judas betrayed the friendship of Christ and yielded to desperate death; Francis, on the contrary, faithful to it, defeated and mocked "sister corporal death".

5. The absolute iconographical apex: the "Minor Christ" of St. Francis

All the mural decoration of the Tau cross body of the Lower basilica found its absolute climax in the triple representation of Christ crucified in the Apse (lost in 1623) and in the arms of the transept. The iconographical absolute primacy is reserved to the humiliated and suffering God of the religious sentiment of Francis.

The insistence of the image and the ample spaces reserved to it, render immediately readable the spiritual importance of this dramatic Gospel page in franciscan ambience. Definitely disanchored from hieratic medieval schemes, it has been brought, owing mainly to "unlearned and illitterate" Francis, on more historical and affective schemes.

"In the Passion of Christ themes - GF HEGEL wrote - the sublime and victorious were no more underlined but only the touching side of them: this was the immediate consequence of that elated inebriatedness of the sentimental partecipation to the pain the Redemptor underwent while on earth, to which Saint Francis had confered a new energy, unknown until then"[31]. It was mainly by proposing such moving image of God that Francis seduced and won the hearts and minds of the Christian crowds as thirsty of God as eager and longing to hear Francis' fervent word.

For the Saint of Assisi the Cross of Christ is the acme of the history of salvation: "If I be lifted up from the earth, will draw all men unto me". In memory of this main salvific image, Francis liked to mark the humble cells, sign the letters and shape his habit in the form of a Tau cross (Fig. 65). For him Christ Crucified was the definite value, the Alpha and Omega of the history of salvation, the pivot point of all his life as a convert: from San Damiano to... La Verna, up to the moment of physical death he met with true paschal joy! From the eloquent walls that enwrap his corporal remains, he insists on proclaiming: "I determined not to know anything among you, brother, save Jesus Christ and him crucified"[32].

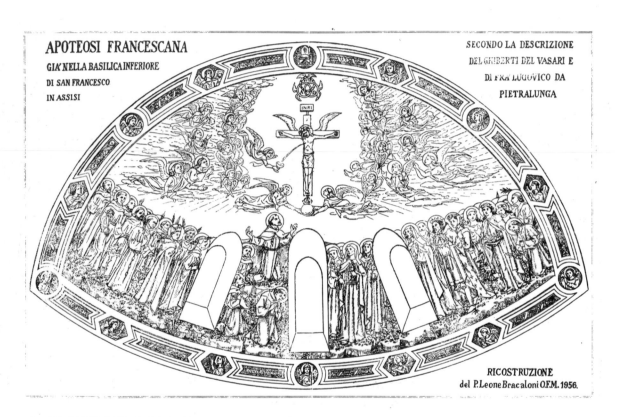

L. BRACALONI (1956): Reconstruction of the lost allegory representing the "Glory of the Crucifix". Ghiberti, Vasari, Lodovico da Pietralunga, Tossignani left us precious descriptions of the frescoe in the apse basin which the author Puccio Capanna had left unfinished.

Essential references

(¹) *Bullarium Franciscanum, I, Romae* 1759, 40

(²) UBERTINUS A CASALE, *Arbor vitae crucifixae, B.V., Ch. 3. (Life of Blessed Giles).*

(³) *Legend of Three Companions, n. 72.*

(⁴) E. FRANCIA, *L'arte paleocristiana,* Milano 1969, 207.

(⁵) *Legenda Major, IV, 2 (Chapter dedicated to humility).*

(⁶) THOMAS OF CELANO, *I and II Lives: nn. 201 and 108 resp.*

(⁷) A. MARINI, *Archivium Franciscanum Historicum,* 73 (1980) 25.

(⁸) CELANO, II, 77: GIORDANO DA GIANO, *Chroniche, n. 50.*

(⁹) E., LEMPP, *Frere Elie de Cortone,* Paris 1901, 78 +.

(¹⁰) SALIMBENE DA PARMA, *Chronicle, in Fonti Francescane (=FF),* Padova 1980, p. 2115.

(¹¹) M. BIHL, *in Arch. Franc. Hist.,* 1 (1980) 653.

(¹²) *Letter on death of Saint Francis, in FF,* 399.

(¹³) Letter to all Custodes, 6; Testament, 13.

(¹⁴) P. SCARPELLINI, *Assisi e i suoi monumenti, in Assisi al tempo di San Francesco,* Assisi 1978, 71 + (*Plates: II, VIII, XII*).

(¹⁵) F. CASOLINI, *Il protomonastero di Santa Chiara,* Milano 1950, 206 + (*Plan and vertical section of burial cell, 216*).

(¹⁶) *Canonization trial, in FF,* 23334.

(¹⁷) *Il libro della Beata Angela da Foligno,* Roma 1950, 26 +.

(¹⁸) *Mirror of Perfection, n. 109.*

(¹⁹) L. BELLOSI, *La barba di SF, in Prospettiva* 22 (1980) 11 +.

(²⁰) S. DA CAMPAGNOLA, *L'angelo del VI° sigillo e l'Alter Christus,* Roma 1971, 292.

(²¹) A. GRABAR, *L'arte paleocristiana,* Milano 1980, 274.

(²²) *Legend Major, Prologue, 1; XIII, 10.*

(²³) AA. VV., *I Frati Minori Conventuali,* Roma 1978, 43 +.

(²⁴) L. DA PIETRALUNGA *left a description of the lost allegory of the Crucifix. See Descrizione della Basilica di SF, in Bollettino di Storia per l'Umbria,* Vol. XXVIII, 47 +.

(²⁵) *Reported by* S. DA CAMPAGNOLA, *op. cit, p. 174.*

(²⁶) CELANO, I, 84.

(²⁷) *Collationes, 185; MIGNE PL 38, 997.*

(²⁸) *Phil. II, 6 +.*

(²⁹) *Op. cit., p. 58.*

(³⁰) THOMAS ECCLESTON, *Chronicle, Conversation XV.*

(³¹) *Reported by* M. HERUBEL, *La pittura gotica, I,* Milano 1967, p. 103 (*Documenti e testimonianze*).

(³²) CELANO, II, 105; *See I Cor. 2,2; Gal. 6,14.*

List of colour Plates

Other literature

I. Historical

Angeli F., Collis Paradisi Amoenitas, Montefiascone 1704.

Lombardi B., Della sepoltura del Serafico Padre dei Minori, Roma 1797.

Guadagni F., De invento Corpore Divi Francisci, Roma 1819; Idem, Sententiae dictae a Procuratoribus Generalibus Familiarum Franciscalium in causa inventi Corporis D. Francisci, Roma 1820.

Fea C., Descrizione ragionata della Sacrosanta Patriarcale Basilica di S. Francesco d'Assisi, Roma 1820.

Fratini G., Storia della Basilica e del Convento di S. Francesco in Assisi, Prato 1882.

Marinangeli B., La tomba di S. Francesco attraverso i secoli, in San Francesco Patrono d'Italia, annate 1920-24.

Di Fonzo L., Francesco d'Assisi, in Bibliotecha Sanctorum, Roma 1964, 1096-1108.

AA. VV. La ricognizione del Corpo di S. Francesco, Spoleto 1978.

II. Iconological and Technical

Kleinschmidt B., Die Basilika SF in Assisi, Berlin 1915-26.

Tantillo Mignosi, A., Osservazioni sul transetto della Basilica inferiore di Assisi, in Bollettino d'Arte, 3/4 (1975) 129-142.

Gosebruch M., Gli affreschi di Giotto nel braccio destro del transetto e nelle vele, in Giotto e Giotteschi, Roma 1972, pp. 129ss.

Bracaloni L., L'arte francescana nella vita e nella storia di settecento anni, Todi 1924; IDEM, La gloria francescana nel grande affresco absidale già in San Francesco d'Assisi, in Studi Francescani, XXXIII (1936) 3-17.

Coletti L., Gli affreschi della Basilica inferiore di Assisi, Bergamo 1949.

Toscano B., Storia dell'arte e forme della vita religiosa, in Storia dell'arte italiana, Torino 1979, 271-318.

Cottier T.P., "Le vele" nella Basilica inferiore di Assisi, Firenze 1981.

5

11

B·IACOBA·EX

13

14

15 ▶

18 19
20

1

2

23
24

27

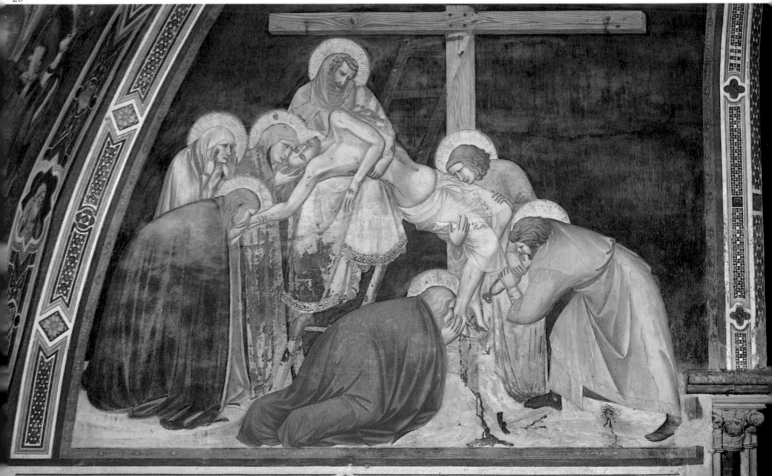

40
41

48

2

FORTITUDO

PENITENTIE

TIMOR

PAVPTAS

SPES

ICPVNGI
SPOSA

EX VERIS BONIS
XPO TRIBUIT

58

59

60

61

62
63

64
65

67
69